the Hidden Garden

A BLESSING BOYS' ADVENTURE

JUSTIN KNOOP

Published by StoryBuilders Press
Hardcover: 978-1-954521-68-1
Paperback: 978-1-954521-69-8
eBook: 978-1-954521-70-4

To my boys: Ty, London, Judah, and Zion.
God has an incredible adventure awaiting each of you.
Trust Him, follow His path, and embrace every moment
with courage and joy.
Love, Dad.

One sunny afternoon, the Blessing Boys—Ty, London, Judah, and Zion—were helping their dad mow their grandma's lawn and cut away the vines growing around her garage.

They'd been working hard all morning. The vines were thick and tough to cut, but they'd cleared enough away that they could see the door again.

Grandma brought out a pitcher of lemonade and a plate of sandwiches for everyone to share under the tall oak tree growing in the backyard.

"This tree has been here since long before your grandfather built our house," Grandma said, setting the tray down.

"I bet it's been here forever!" Zion exclaimed.

Grandma patted Zion on the head. "That's just what your grandfather said. You boys enjoy those sandwiches. Your father and I will be inside if you need anything."

As Judah took a bite of his bologna, an acorn hit him on the top of his head and landed in the grass behind him.

"Ouch!" he said, feeling the tender spot under his hair. He turned around to see where the acorn had landed and noticed something shiny sticking out of the ground. He pulled out an old, dusty bottle containing a rolled-up map.

"Look what I found!"

Judah shouted.

Ty carefully unrolled the map. It showed a path through their town leading to a place marked with a star.

"It's a treasure map!"

Judah said, his eyes sparkling with excitement.

"Maybe this is God's way of leading us to something special," London suggested. "Tomorrow morning, let's see where it leads."

The next day, Ty, London, and Judah gathered their supplies for the treasure hunt. Zion walked into the kitchen, his backpack ready to go.

"Zion, I don't think you can come with us this first time," Ty said.

"But I was there when you found the map," he cried.

"We don't know where this is leading us, though. We want to make sure the way is safe before you come," Ty added.

Zion took off his backpack, his shoulders slumped. "Can I at least pray with you before you leave?"

Ty smiled. "Of course. You can always pray with us, Zion. And when we know what this star is, we promise to take you there."

The brothers stood in a circle and grabbed hands.

"Zion, would you do the honors?" London asked.

"Dear, Jesus, thank you for this day. Thank you for my brothers, and please watch out for them on their adventure and keep them safe. And please help them find something cool to show me. Amen."

The Blessing Boys set out to follow the map. They walked through the familiar streets of their neighborhood, past the old park, and into the woods behind their town.

The map led them to a hidden path covered with ivy and bushes.
"We have to clear the way," Ty said.

"It looks like no one has been here for years."

"Good thing we had so much practice at Grandma's house yesterday," Judah laughed.

London and Ty worked together to move a fallen log out of the path. Judah trimmed back overgrown bushes and cleaned up litter that had been caught in some of the branches.

When they were done, they could see a trail winding back into the forest.

"This looks like the dotted line on the map!" London said excitedly. "I think we're close to the star!"

"Let's keep going,"

Ty said, leading the way.

As they ventured deeper into the woods, the path led them to a clearing with a giant tree in the middle. It was so large, the boys couldn't see the top.

Suddenly, a squirrel scampered down the tree and stood before them.

"Welcome, Blessing Boys! My name is Squeaky. I'm the protector of this forest. I've been waiting for someone to find the lost map. It leads to a special hidden garden. But beware; it's protected by puzzles and challenges!"

Squeaky led the brothers past the tree to the first challenge:

a large

hedge

maze.

"To reach the garden, you must find your way through the Maze of Distraction," Squeaky explained. "Inside you'll find temptations to pull you from your purpose. Stay strong in your faith and your quest to make it through."

"How will we know which way to go?" Ty asked Squeaky, but the squirrel had disappeared as quickly as he'd come.

"What do we do now?" London asked.

"Trust in the Lord with all your heart and lean not on your own understanding," Judah quoted Proverbs 3:5.

"The only way to the hidden garden is through the maze."

Ty, London, and Judah entered the maze. Right away they found things they liked to do, things easier than solving a giant maze. But if they were going to find the garden and show it to Zion, they would have to stay focused and rely on God to lead them.

Working together, they solved the twists and turns, encouraging each other to stay focused on the task God had given them.

When they exited the maze, Squeaky was waiting for them.

"Great job, Blessing Boys!

You kept going even
when it was hard.

The last thing you have to do is cross the Bridge of Courage.
Then you'll be in the hidden garden. See you there!"

With that, Squeaky was gone again.

The brothers stood at the edge of a cliff watching the rickety bridge sway over a deep ravine.

London hesitated.

"It's okay, London," Ty said. "Here's what I do when I'm scared."

Ty closed his eyes and prayed,

"Lord, please give us courage and keep us safe. Amen."

"And we'll hold your hand," Judah said, smiling.

Together, they crossed the bridge, supporting each other along the way.

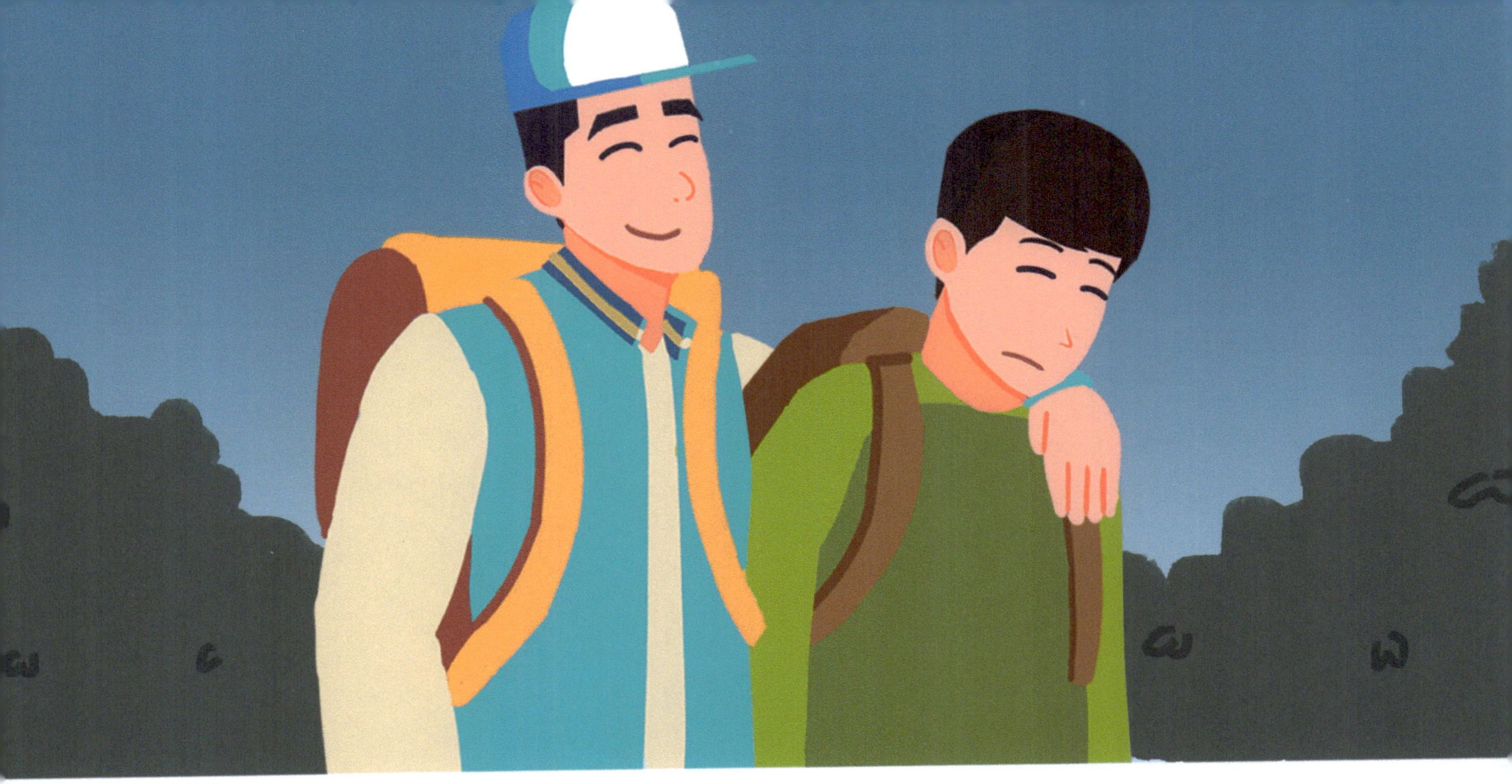

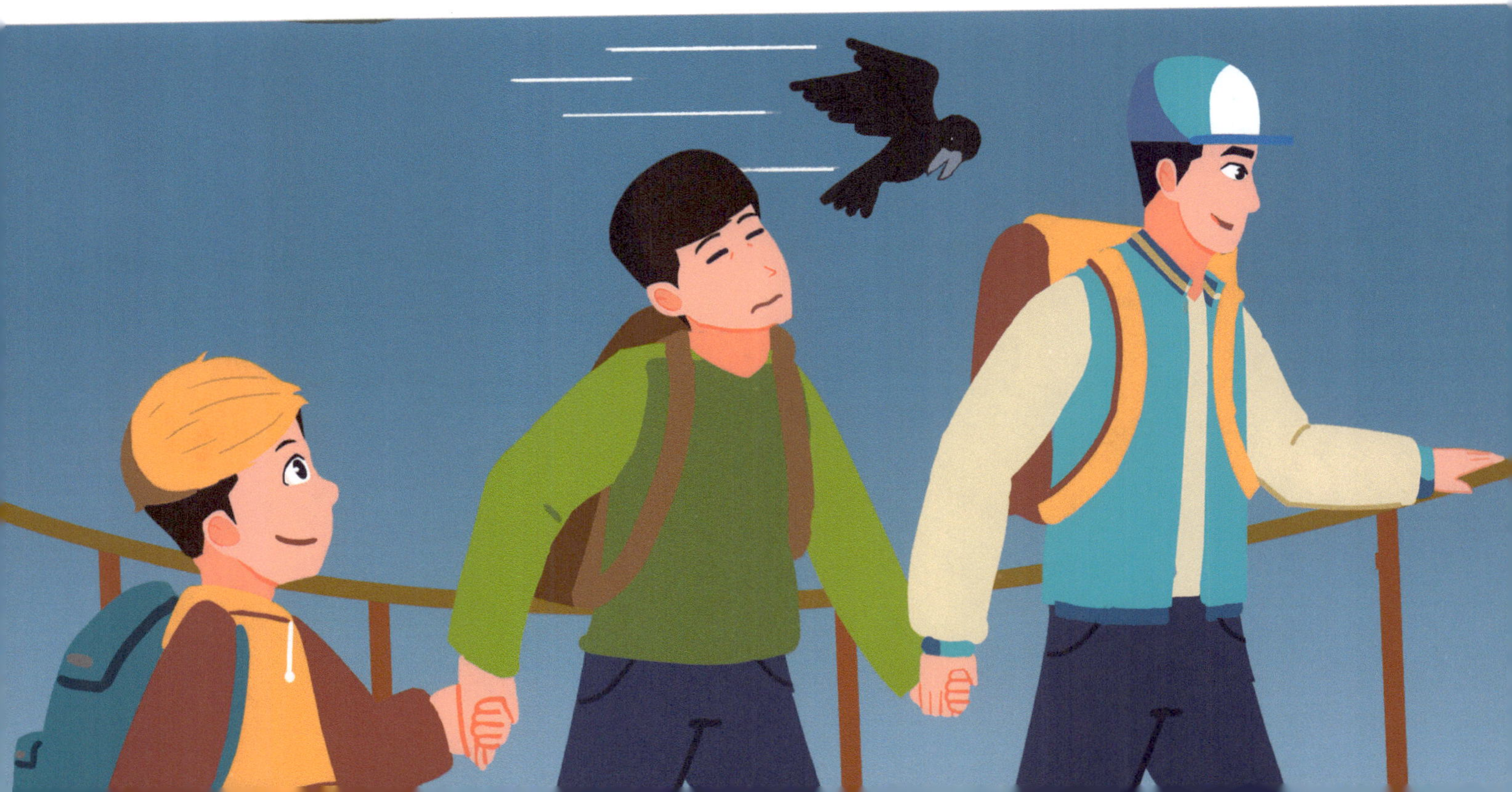

On the other side of the bridge, Ty, London, and Judah reached the hidden garden.

Once a place of immaculate beauty, vibrant plants, and creatures of all kinds, the garden had become overgrown.

In fact, the fountain in the center of the garden was covered in so many leaves and vines that the water could no longer flow.

Squeaky jumped down from one of the branches near London and Judah.

"This garden was created to bring joy and beauty to the world," he said, "but no one has been here for a long time. Will you be the new caretakers and make the garden beautiful again?"

"This looks like a really hard job," London said.

"It does look like a lot of work, but through Christ, all things are possible!" Ty exclaimed.

"And if we work together, we can do anything," Judah added.

The Blessing Boys got right to work clearing away the brush and vines from the fountain.

As soon as London pulled the last bit of leaves out of the basin, water bubbled out of the top and fell down, filling the bowl.

Squeaky ran over and took a drink of the water.

"Thank you, Blessing Boys! Now the animals who live here will have fresh water to drink again."

The boys were so excited, they made quick work of trimming the bushes and cleaning up the rest of the garden before heading home.

Zion was waiting for his brothers on the front porch of their house and jumped up when he saw them. He was excited to hear all about their adventure, and he couldn't wait to meet Squeaky for himself. But his brothers' work in the hidden garden had given him an idea.

"Remember that park by Grandma's house? The one with the broken swings? What if we cleaned it up like you did in the hidden garden? If kids could play there again, maybe it wouldn't be empty all the time," Zion said.

"Zion! What a great project!" Ty said.

"Can I come this time?" Zion asked.

"You certainly can," Ty answered. "In fact, I think you should be team leader. It was your idea after all."

"I second that," London said.

As the Blessing Boys cleaned up the park near their grandma's house, some of the neighbors came out to help.

Zion showed the smaller kids how to pull weeds and plant flowers, while the bigger kids fixed the swingset. After a couple of hours, it looked like a brand new park.

The boys rested quietly under a tree near the slide when Grandma came over to see them.

"Your hard work and faith make this world a better place. Look at what you've been able to do!"

she said. " 'Whatever you do, work at it with all your heart, as working for the Lord.' Do you know where that comes from?"

"Colossians chapter 3, verse 23," the boys replied.

"That's right.

You've shown yourselves to be great servants of the Lord," she said.

"I can't wait to see what He has in store for us next!" Zion said.

Join the Adventure

The Blessings Boys invite you to become a Blessing Buddy and join them in making the whole world as beautiful as the hidden garden. God gave us the gift of the Earth and taking care of it is one way to glorify Him and show our thanks for what He's given us.

There are many ways to help out: clean up a park, help a neighbor or grandparent cut their grass, plant a tree or flowers, or pick up litter. Together, we can create a world as beautiful as the garden the boys discovered.

Remember, "Let your light shine before others, that they may see your good deeds and glorify your Father in heaven," Matthew 5:16. Join the Blessing Boys in their adventure, and be a part of the change!

Follow us on Social

@theblessingboys

Subscribe and follow us for upcoming
News and Future books

www.ingramcontent.com/pod-product-compliance
Lightning Source LLC
Chambersburg PA
CBHW041431120626
46547CB00002B/167